Being Selfish

Joy Berry
Illustrated by Bartholomew

Joy Berry Books
New York

This book is about Katie and her friend, Sam.

Reading about Katie and Sam can help you understand and deal with being selfish.

Have you ever been with people who would not share their food with you?

Have you ever played with people who would not share their toys with you?

People who do not share are selfish.

They care more about themselves than about others.

When you are with someone who is selfish, how do you feel?

What do you think?

What do you do?

When you are with someone who is selfish,
you might feel left out, frustrated, and angry.

You might not want to be with that person.

It is important to treat others the way you want to be treated.

If you want others to share with you, you need to share with them.

You need to be unselfish.

Being unselfish does not mean that you have to share all your things all the time.

Sometimes you cannot share.

Put the food away if you do not have enough to share.

Try not to eat in front of someone who does not have anything to eat.

Try to be fair if you are going to share. Here is a good rule for dividing something.

Let one person divide.

Let the other person choose.

You might not want to share something that is special to you.

Do not use the special thing in front of someone else, unless:
- The person does not want to use it.
- The person has something else to use.

You do not have to share with anyone who is careless.

Put your things away if you think they might be lost or damaged.

You can help other people take care of the things you share with them by doing these things.

Show them how your things work.

Show them how to take care of your things.

Be fair if there is only one of something that must be shared by two or more people.

Take turns using it.

Let each person use it for an equal length of time. You can use a clock or timer to help keep track of the time.

If you want to be happy, you should treat other people the way you want to be treated.

This means you should not be selfish because you do not want other people around you to be selfish.

Joy Berry Enterprises
146 West 29th St., Suite 11RW
New York, NY 10001

Cover Design & Art Direction: John Bellaud
Cover Illustration & Art Production: Geoff Glisson

Production Location: HX Printing, Guangzhou, China
Date of Production: February 2010
Cohort: Batch 1

Printed in China
ISBN 978-1-60577-133-5